# THE ARCHITECTS
## OF HOPE

# THE ARCHITECTS
# OF HOPE

SIXTEEN YOUNG PEOPLE
DREAMING OF A BETTER TOMORROW

## ARI SATOK

The Architects of Hope:
Sixteen Young People Dreaming of a Better Tomorrow
1st Edition

ISBN: 978-0-9978435-0-7

To reach the author, please email thearchitectsofhope@gmail.com.

## *Dedication*

To the wonderful uwc communities that I worked with, whose openness and warmth made this book possible.

# Contents

# Introduction

In January of 2014, I was on a visit to an international boarding school in South Wales, the second of four school visits as part of a research project I was conducting for my undergraduate thesis. Housed in a 12th-century castle, the school I was visiting sat on a campus overlooking the Bristol Channel. A centuries-old entrance gate still stood, as if to preserve the castle's isolation, and the dramatic sea cliffs along the Channel seemed only to intensify the feeling of seclusion. On the campus's sprawling grounds, serenity was everywhere.

Inside the castle walls, though, was a far less tranquil world, where high school students from all corners of the globe walked through a maze of hallways and staircases, darting in and out of meetings and classes. They walked with the bearing of busyness, guided from room to room by a seemingly never-ending marathon of commitments. But every day, at lunch and at dinner, the pace briefly slowed as students gathered together for meals in the castle's magnificent dining hall.

As a visitor, I loved those meals. Each lunch and dinner played host to conversations that fascinated me: conversations in which the nearly 90 countries represented by the student body came alive as stories. Sometimes, I sat at tables with students from as many countries as there were seats. And all I had to do to enter the worlds from which they came was listen.

One dinner, I sat with a student named Mira from Syria. At the time, I knew almost nothing about the civil war decimating her country and its civilians; it was little more than a tragic headline to me. While we ate, Mira told me her story. Long after we cleared our plates and the dining hall's kitchen closed for the night, I was still sitting with her, hearing her haunting tale of devastation and dislocation: the tale of a girl who had lost her home. She recounted the terror of standing frozen on a street corner as the street around the bend was being shelled, the fear that came with hearing the sounds of gunfire, the sadness of leaving behind a neighborhood that had always been hers. But there was still a hope within her, however faint, that one day the civil war would end. By the time we parted ways, a country and a conflict had a human face.

I left that conversation compelled by an urge to share Mira's story. I couldn't have fully explained then why sharing Mira's story somehow felt necessary; I just knew that it did. What I did not know was that in that urge was the seed of an idea that would guide the next two years of my life.

* * *

During my freshman year of university, a few years before meeting Mira, I was first introduced to the United World College (UWC) movement of international schools, of which Mira's school was a part. More than 50 years ago, an educational visionary named Kurt Hahn imagined the movement into existence. Education, he believed, was the force that could bridge the divide between young people experiencing the political conflict of the Cold War. If they lived and learned in the same community, he reasoned, they would surely break down prejudices and build bridges of peace. It was a bold vision, but Hahn was not one to shy away from audacious dreams. And so, in a castle on the sea – the castle in which I met Mira – the dream of a school became a reality.

The school attracted 16- to 20-year-olds from all around the world, who, together, completed their high school educations and immersed themselves in activities aimed at helping them share their cultures and build a community. As years went by, educators from across the globe heard about this experiment in education and decided to create their own versions. On Vancouver Island, a second United World College school was born. In Singapore, a third was added, in the Kingdom of Swaziland, a fourth. An experiment grew into a movement.

I first heard about the movement from my classmates at Princeton University. I was an international student and came to know a number of United World College graduates within the international student community. At the time, there were 12 UWC schools (at the time of this publication there are 16), and as I met classmates who had attended UWC schools and started hearing stories about their high schools, I grew fascinated by the movement. I was surprised by the movement's size; UWC claims over 60,000 alumni from more than 180 countries. I was enthralled by the schools' diversity; each school draws students from dozens of countries, many of them attending on full financial scholarships. But mostly, I was enchanted by the almost fairy tale-like quality that each school seemed to evoke; they seemed like places where all things were possible.

As I progressed through university and reached senior year, my interest in these schools continued to grow. I became so interested, in fact, that I decided to make the United World College movement the subject of my senior thesis. I read all the material on the movement I could find. I interviewed graduates. And then, funded by my university, I visited four of the movement's schools to try to understand how they impacted their students.

I met Mira in Wales on the second of these four visits, each one to a different UWC campus. The first visit was to Canada, the third to Italy, the fourth to Bosnia and Herzegovina. During each school visit, I talked to students and faculty, tagged along to student activities, and sat in on classes, in which students with myriad English accents debated and discussed big ideas. The more that I traveled, the more Miras I met: remarkably articulate students whose stories embodied, or at the very least evoked, all sorts of social issues and realities. Each school felt like a library of unwritten stories: an anthology of the experience of youth around the world that no one had yet compiled. An idea sparked within me. What if I endeavored to create it?

As I contemplated the idea more, I felt an increasing desire to make it happen. I finished my thesis, and in the months that immediately followed, I worked to turn what had begun as an abstract dream into a concrete vision. It was a vision to return to some of the movement's schools, gather the stories of its students and then share them far beyond the walls of each campus. If each campus was a symphony of human experience, my job would be to make those symphonies loud enough for the world to hear.

# INTRODUCTION

The motivation for the project was simple. In Mira's story, and in the countless I heard as I continued my research, I felt a tremendous power. It was more than just a narrative power, the quality that makes readers turn to the next page of a book, or listeners hang on to every syllable of a story. It was the power of inspiration and of perspective.

Each story I was hearing was a portal into a new world that I previously knew nothing about, an invitation to learn about a country, culture, and way of life foreign to my own. A chasm of differences might stand between countries, but stories, I was convinced, could bring them together. They could allow us to see ourselves in the lives of others. They could shed from us ignorance we did not realize we possessed, and turn stereotypes into understandings. They could help us see and care about the world beyond our borders in all its nuance and humanity. Stories were powerful, I believed, and so I sought to capture them.

I shared my vision with a number of United World College schools and was granted the opportunity to spend extended time – anywhere from two to five weeks – in residence at their schools, to work with their students and communities. I shared the vision with a funder, and was blessed with a generous grant. In the spirit of United World College, an idea had become a reality.

For close to one year, I traveled to seven schools throughout the movement, immersing myself in the stories I found at each. I began my journey by returning to the Canadian campus on Vancouver Island, nestled in the woods along the shores of a picturesque bay. From there, I traveled to the Hong Kong UWC, a pleasantly spacious campus in a metropolis that is a forest of skyscrapers. I spent time at three campuses in Europe: one in Freiburg, Germany, on the site of an ancient monastery, another in Maastricht, Netherlands, and the last in Llantwit Major, Wales, in that dazzling castle by the sea. I visited a campus in Montezuma, New Mexico, housed in its own castle, a converted 19th-century hotel overflowing with charm. And I completed my travels at the campus in the Kingdom of Swaziland, a revolutionary school in southern Africa that had the boldness to racially integrate its student body during the years of apartheid.

# INTRODUCTION

The settings were widely varied, but in each I found what I had discovered on my first visit to Wales: students from dozens of countries with stories to share. During my visits I interviewed nearly 150 students from almost 100 different countries. For me, these interviews were a tremendous learning opportunity. For the students, they were a platform through which to share and educate. And for the eventual audience, it was my hope that my project would become a window into the world in all its mesmerizing diversity.

\* \* \*

At first, I produced most students' stories as audio pieces — oral portraits of their personal narratives. In the middle of my journey, I began to experiment with another medium of storytelling: poetry. I wrote poetry stories — rhyming narratives, each of which captured an individual student's life experiences — as well as shorter poems, each of which captured a specific moment in a student's life. It was, no doubt, an unconventional form of storytelling, but as I shared these poems and poetry stories, it became clear that they were striking a chord with my readers. Accordingly, I have since directed most of my energies into writing more of these poems and poetry stories. This book is a collection of them.

The selection of the poems in this collection centers on the theme of hope: searching for it, finding it, losing it. Few themes within my interviews seemed more universal. For hope, though infinite in the forms it can take, speaks in all languages and cultures.

This collection introduces you to a group of remarkable young people, whose stories all relate to this idea of hope. In the stories of Kainat from Pakistan, who was shot by the Taliban in their quest to suppress girls' education, and of Sibia, from Guatemala, who grew up all too aware of her country's glaring educational inequalities, is the common hope for equality. In the stories of Aiham from Syria, who witnessed his country's implosion, and Uddhav, from Nepal, who watched from afar as his country was brought to its knees by an earthquake, is the yearning to hope for a brighter tomorrow in the bleakness of a devastated present. In the stories of Arudi, from Kenya, who spent a year in New York, raising her voice through the Black Lives Matter movement, and of Killaq, an indigenous student from Iqaluit in Northern Canada, who has spent years standing up for the lives of indigenous people and the preservation of their culture, is a shared hope for dignity and respect.

The collection, when taken as a whole, makes no simple claims about hope. Hope, in its infinite varieties, has no one outcome, nor is it always possible. But often, in the face of adversity – racism, natural disaster, war, poverty, and so many other problems that persist in the world – hope is what enables action and what lets us conquer tragedy and hardship.

When I look back at my journey through the United World College movement, hope has been the guiding theme. It was hope that brought the movement's first school together more than a half-century ago. It was hope that caused school after school to sprout and grow in its image. And it is hope that hums, even if sometimes in the face of great pain, in the beautiful web of stories, traded each night in a Gothic dining hall in a castle on the sea, where all things seem possible. This collection is that hope.

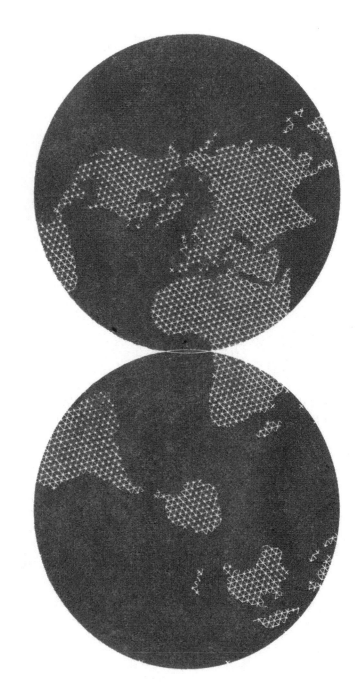

## The Architects of Hope

HERE live the architects of hope
Sketching blueprints of tomorrows
Still unseen today
Whose plans call not
For bricks or steel
For hope is built of different things
Of little dreams
Stacked one by one
Towards the sky
Until they one day reach it

# Sibia

Sibia grew up in Chimaltenango, Guatemala. One of her fondest childhood memories is of participating in the National Science Olympiad, an annual competition that brings together some of the brightest science students in the country.

Three years in a row she competed, and three years in a row she made it to the contest's final round, held in Guatemala City. Her community was shocked by her successes. Most of her co-competitors were from significantly better-resourced schools in the capital city; for a girl from outside the capital to make it to the finals, and then repeat the accomplishment two more times, was extremely uncommon.

For Sibia, these competitions were living lessons on the power of determination. "When you are passionate about something," she says, "do not use the fact that you don't have resources as a barrier. Take it as an inspiration." It's a lesson she tries to mold her life around and this poem tells the story of another adventure in Sibia's life that that lesson propelled: her dream to study abroad.

# The Weightlessness of Dreaming

THERE's a beautiful time as a child
When no dream is too large to sustain
When the limits that seek to restrict us
Have yet to make war on the brain

For the demons of doubt have not fashioned
All the armies of fear don't exist
Insecurities' warriors lie dormant
For they've yet to have cause to enlist

In this peacetime, a child can smile from the heart
For her life is untarnished by strife;
She can hold on her shoulders a million dreams
For her living's unburdened by life

*   *   *

In a small town within Guatemala
One such child named Sibia grows up;
The more that she opens her eyes to the world
The more that its beauty shows up

She sees cornfields that span the horizon
She sees orchards where fruits line the ground
She looks up to the sky in its unending blue
In which rainbows of birds can be found

She sees mountains, as if carved by sculptors,
Ornamented with myriad plants
And she knows in the distance are forests
Full of monkeys and jaguars and ants

In her own town, she walks through the market
In which grandmothers peddle their stories
Every Sunday she notices churches
That seem bathed in faith's infinite glories

# SIBIA

And to her, life feels charged with potential –
There is nothing that she cannot be
In a world in which weights often ground us
The young girl lives weightlessly free

* * *

Yet, that state of incomparable lightness
As she grows up takes on greater weight
Childhood may feel like it's eternal
But in real life it has an end date

When its rose-colored glasses grow blurry
Then replaced by new lenses of youth;
It is then the girl grasps that her once-younger self
Lived life missing one difficult truth:

Even beautiful things can be blemished
In invisible, unnoticed ways;
There are stains even if unapparent
Underneath beauty's radiant haze

With this knowledge, she sees in her country
Flaws that childhood helped her ignore
She sees people who face major struggles
Whom she never had noticed before

In the cornfields where once she saw beauty
She sees children who don't go to school
And she wonders, as she spots them working,
Why the way of the world can seem cruel

Sibia's heart breaks when she sees these children
For she knows their lives could have been hers
When she thinks about their likely futures
Deep within her, a vast sadness stirs

# THE WEIGHTLESSNESS OF DREAMING

Yet, what leaves Sibia even more saddened
Is in schools where the mind should be fed
Most like her, who do get education
View their schooling as something to dread

The best teachers are constantly leaving,
Inspiration's exceedingly rare,
And as students grow older and older
About school, they decreasingly care

Sibia's bothered by all the indifference
She's dismayed that her school seems so flawed
But a high schooler can't fix her high school
So she dreams to go study abroad

For abroad, she'll escape the indifference
That she feels, at her school, is the norm
And perhaps, she'll acquire the skills that she needs
To help schools in her country reform

She imagines herself on an airplane
Taking flight to a new foreign school;
These are thoughts in her mind of a dreamer
Though to others, they're thoughts of a fool

"Does she realize," she hears in the whispers
Of the locals who live in her town
"That her dream will not likely be realized,
That she likely will end up let down?

Does she not understand how few students
From our town have been sent overseas?
Does she know that a scholarship isn't a thing
That one's given with relative ease?"

# SIBIA

Sibia hears all these whispers and panics
For the demons of doubt in her rise;
Insecurities' warriors awaken
As they ambush her hopes by surprise

But the captains of hope catch their bearings
Optimism's commanders reset
Though they see that their fight won't be easy
They have faith they can outlast the threat

For they know that a dream has more ammo
Than the gloom it is forced to fight back
With the doubt that now battles their borders
It's with faith that they counterattack

It's a counterattack led by courage
That takes charge within Sibia's brain
She's reminded her dream to go study abroad
Is a dream she has hope to attain

So she fights for her dream and attains it
She's accepted to study abroad
All the people who thought that her dreams were too big
As they watch her departure are awed

But for her this is only a short-term goodbye
For she leaves with a clear-sighted plan
Though she'll live in a world far away from her own
She'll return home whenever she can

\*   \*   \*

That chance comes her first summer vacation
She takes it without second thought
She signs up to help a remote rural school
Where indigenous children are taught

# THE WEIGHTLESSNESS OF DREAMING

First, she translates and works in the kitchen
Then a chance to help teach comes her way
She runs workshops in arts education
And leads students in music and play

With her smile, she lights up the classroom
For each student, she desperately cares
And her story of chasing an unlikely dream
Is a story she frequently shares

All her students are moved by her story
In their futures it lets them believe
When the summer is close to concluding
They're all sad Sibia soon has to leave

But before she departs they inform her
"We dream one day to be just like you:
 To go study abroad and to travel
But to come back to help our home too"

Sibia smiles to hear such ambitions
On the last day before she departs
In return, she shares with them one insight
That she hopes will remain in their hearts:

"Hold on tight," she says, "to today's feelings
When no dream feels too large to sustain
And resist all the limits and boundaries
That will one day make war on the brain

For this beautiful time as a child
Is the wisest that you'll ever be
Live your life on the wings of your most daring dreams
And you'll live feeling weightlessly free"

# *Aiham*

Aiham grew up in Damascus, Syria. Though he has long since left, he can still picture the Syria of his childhood, beneath the one haunted by death and devastation that the media captures today. He remembers lively shisha cafes, echoing with laughter and conversation. He remembers the old city, with its ancient gates, snaking alleyways and traditional Arab houses. And he remembers hearing stories of a site just outside of Damascus that always fascinated him: a mountain that locals believe is where Cain murdered Abel in the biblical story. Aiham claims that on a stone wall inside one of the mountain's many caves is what appears to be a huge screaming face. "The mountain went screaming because it was the first murder on earth," Aiham explained of the mythology behind the cave.

Millennia later, the story of Cain and Abel has an eerie resonance in modern day Syria, where killing has become commonplace as a devastating civil war continues to turn countrymen into enemies. This poem, addressed to the omnipresent mountain and imagined in Aiham's voice, relates Aiham's experience living in Syria as the country descended into chaos.

# The Eternal Mountain

MOUNTAIN, I know you've seen blood shed
When Cain murdered Abel you screamed
What did you feel as the earth bled
A blood that with strong hatred streamed?

Mountain, when Abel's blood hardened
The mark of his death left a stain
Can sins, in your worldview, be pardoned,
If there's no way to undo their pain?

Mountain, I ask you these questions
For their answers may be mine as well
I look to the world for suggestions
Are there ways to hold hope amidst hell?

\* \* \*

Mountain, the hell I reside in
Was a comfortable place as a child
I wonder, did you once take pride in
The years in which Syria smiled?

Mountain, you saw my Damascus
In its glory before its decay
Do memories let history task us
With its stories that now fade away?

Mountain, we lived in an imperfect peace
But a flawed peace is better than war
Did you imagine our quiet would cease
And be filled with war's terrible roar?

Mountain, few people remember
The day revolution began
Were you told in that fateful December
Of the actions of one outraged man?

# AIHAM

Mountain, that man in Tunisia
Felt harassed by abuse undeserved
Were his leaders all cursed with amnesia
In forgetting the people they served?

Mountain, the man was a vendor
And the government seized all he sold
Should a man who'd been shamed just surrender
To the laws that his leaders controlled?

Mountain, in protest, the young man
Set his tormented body aflame
Do you think revolution was his plan
Or, perhaps, just an end to his shame?

Mountain, regardless the answer
His example gave voice to new dreams
Did you see how his rage, like a cancer,
With great speed, spread to other regimes?

Mountain, there were protests and rallies
From Yemen, across to Algeria
Could you hear from our streets and our alleys
That the fervor would soon come to Syria?

Mountain, they called it the great "Arab Spring"
Greater freedoms and rights in its goals
Did you too imagine the protests would bring
A change in our region's controls?

Mountain, perhaps I was blinded
I saw just the Spring's hope, not its curse
In our present, are you too reminded
Revolution can make a place worse?

# THE ETERNAL MOUNTAIN

Mountain, a still peaceful tension
Would quickly evolve into war
Did you also have no comprehension
Of the scale of the violence in store?

Mountain, we thought all would calm down
That the tension and mistrust would mend
How did we then have our hopes drown
Into chaos with no clear-cut end?

Mountain, a war, first two-sided
Into myriad sides would soon splinter
Could you tell as the country divided
That the "Spring" would transform into winter?

Mountain, peace talks were forsaken
It was simpler to kill than to talk
Do you still scream when human life's taken,
Or have life's horrors robbed you of shock?

Mountain, each death birthed another
An eye for an eye made us blind
Would the true keeper of his own brother
Not feel brotherhood to all mankind?

Mountain, the streets became wild
From my house, I was soon sent away
Could you hear my dad tell me: "My child
In our home it's too risky to stay"

Mountain, I moved to my aunt's place
But the war's chaos followed me there
Is it possible to keep a strong face
When the sounds of war hang in the air?

# AIHAM

Mountain, one night raged a long fight
On our street, there were gunshots and blasts
What do you do through that long night
When you think that night will be your last?

Mountain, I learned what I'd long known
In this hell, life was only survival
Have you wished that you could leave this warzone
In the years since this long war's arrival?

Mountain, my father decided
It was time for my family to leave
Can one live in a country divided
And to normalcy still try to cleave?

Mountain, I wish that the answer was yes
But I now can accept that it's no
Do you think that my future will still hold distress
As away from my country I go?

Mountain, no matter the hardship I'll deal
With my future's uncertain tomorrows
But tell me in truth – does the heart ever heal
When it's buried in mountains of sorrows?

Mountain, I look at this once-wondrous land
And I ready myself to depart
When will this battle have reached its last stand
And when will the rebuilding start?

Mountain, I ask you these questions
For your answers may be mine as well
I look to the world for suggestions
Are there ways to find hope amidst hell?

# *Nana*

Nana grew up in Accra, Ghana, living there until 2009 when he and his family moved to France for three years. Growing up Christian, he recalls his childhood in Ghana as one characterized by religious tolerance. At school, many of Nana's classmates were Muslims. "It's so beautiful," he remembers, "how Muslims and Christians in Ghana tend to live together peacefully." From his childhood in Ghana, he learned the power of tolerance; from a few incidents in his neighborhood in France, he learned the dangers of its absence. This poem tells the story of the lessons Nana learned from that time in France.

# The Unforgotten Roots

"TAKE pride in your homeland," they told him
"Remember the place where you're from–
  The sounds and the sights, the mornings and nights,
  Let them guide you as you go become

  A child abroad in a new foreign land
  Let your roots hold you up, make you strong,
  And do not forget," they all told him,
"It is here you will always belong

  Though to France you now are heading
  With your family you'll arrive
  Young Nana, from Ghana, remember:
  Keep your memories of Ghana alive"

*  *  *

"I will," young Nana answered
"A home's a home for life,"
  He said with no idea
  That a home could lead to strife

  When it looked and sounded different
  Than the home that others knew
  When he was of different ancestry
  Of a different color too

  For in France, in Nana's neighborhood,
  There were few who shared his race
  Just as few who could identify
  With the struggles he would face

  There was no way to avoid his roots
  There was no way to forget
  For his skin that spoke of heritage
  To others spoke of threat

# THE UNFORGOTTEN ROOTS

To be black, sometimes, was to be felt
To sense a neighbor's fear
To live inside of judgment
That would never disappear

To be made to feel that blackness
Should not be a point of pride
But a heritage and history
That instead should be denied

"Do not deny that heritage
Do not forget your roots"
Said his elders: "Roots grow into trees
And trees one day bear fruits

Though others do not see those fruits
Nor do they see a tree
Don't blame them and don't shame them
But, rather – help them see

Since it's ignorance not insolence
That obscures those future fruits
That makes others see just dirt and mud
Instead of growing roots"

"I won't," young Nana told himself
"My roots won't be denied
My African identity
Will be a source of pride"

And so, when three years later
Back to Ghana, Nana went
He had a new appreciation
For his African descent

# NANA

To be black was to be proud
Not to be felt or to be feared
Blackness could be celebrated
Respected and revered

"There will still come times of disrespect,"
Nana's elders' voices said
"But when it comes, don't bow your head
But hold it up instead

Don't let the traits that others choose
Upon you to project
Impact your sense of dignity
Or worth, or self-respect

Hold on to all you know is true
As you walk upon your path;
Look to leaders who faced prejudice
With love instead of wrath"

\* \* \*

"I will look to them," young Nana said
"How they led in calm and stress
What tactics led to failure?
And what tactics found success?"

First, he learned about Mandela
Then he learned of MLK\*
Then he learned of others from his race
Who held tremendous sway

# THE UNFORGOTTEN ROOTS

As he learned, a dream was born within
To one day lead as well
In his country and his continent
That in his heart both dwell

And he hopes to lead with courage
And a great pride in his roots
For he knows that roots turn into trees
And trees one day bear fruits

*MLK — *Martin Luther King Jr.*

# Arthur

Arthur grew up in São Paulo, Brazil. He was active in the widespread protests that swept through the country in 2013. Ostensibly, the protests were a response to increased bus fares. In reality, Arthur explained, they articulated a much wider range of frustrations. One such frustration was the country's socioeconomic inequalities. This poem tells the story of a particularly poignant moment in which Arthur became aware of these glaring inequalities.

NOTE: *A favela is a Brazilian slum.*

# The Pools of Blood and Water

A young man sees a photograph
And in its frozen story
Is a plot he's seen too many times before

For caught within the camera's eye
An apartment reaches for the sky
While down below
A favela cannot lift itself
Much higher than the ground

Upon the building's balconies
Are swimming pools in which the wealthy swim;
Within the slum below
The only pools
Are those of blood
Its violence each day leaves behind

Between the pools of luxury and those of spilled-out lives
A fence stands guard
To try to keep the worlds apart

Its holes are large enough through which to see the other side
But small enough to claim one can't

\* \* \*

Within this frozen photograph
The young man sees a world reflected in his own
He too lives in São Paulo
He has seen its walls and fences
Carve one city into many more than that

And though the world from which he comes
Is not a world of swimming pools that overflow
Nor of favela water taps that oft run dry;
His mind can't help but wonder
What a life in slums or splendor would be like

What would it be
To lounge beside the swimming pools
To be a child born atop the world
And likely never have to leave?

What would it be
To stand around the pools of blood
To be a child born into chaotic streets
And likely stay within those streets for life?

What would it be to live afraid of those below
In fortresses one calls a home?

What would it be to live afraid of those above
In streets in which police too often hurt instead of help?

What would it take,
He wonders,
For the children of the slums and of the swimming pools
To not live in two cities
Inside one?

What would it take,
He wonders,
For this photograph
To tell a story
Long-lost in the past
And not a living one
That each day
Tells itself anew?

# THE POOLS OF BLOOD AND WATER

The photograph stares up at him
No answers in its world awash with questions
But in questions
Every answer starts
And so he asks
In hopes to find
A future in his city
With no fences and no pools of blood
A photograph of fantasy
A frozen story with a plot
He dreams to one day see

# Kainat

Kainat grew up in Swat Valley, Pakistan. On October 9, 2012, she was riding a school bus on her way home from school after an exam when the bus was attacked. The target of the attack was Kainat's schoolmate, Malala, an activist for girls' education whose voice had been growing in the global community. Malala was brutally shot; in the frenzied chaos of the attack, so too were Kainat and another schoolmate.

Until the attack, Kainat had been a normal girl in Swat Valley, living a life of quiet courage under the Taliban's regime. In the attack's immediate aftermath, she transformed into a symbol of the fight against the Taliban and became a voice for girls' education worldwide. This poem tells her story and speaks to an idea she shared about the other girls in her country: "They want to become something," she said. "They want to become a doctor, or an engineer or a journalist." One day, she believes, they will.

# The Bullet that Turned to a Spark

WHEN nature gave the world its gifts
Some common, others rare,
Swat Valley, in North Pakistan,
Received more than its share

Its meadows buzzed and hummed with life
Its lakes were perfect blue
And mighty mountains seemed to watch
The valley's gifts accrue

In this playground built from nature
In which dreams and hopes could roam
Lived a quiet girl named Kainat
In a warm and loving home

With a dream to be a doctor
To heal and mend and teach
No future for a girl in Swat
To her seemed out of reach

\* \* \*

Each day to school she'd venture
Where a group of girls would learn
Without even an inkling
That the future soon would turn

Down a dark and petrifying path
As the Taliban came in
With claims defining righteousness
And laws defining sin

All the women in the valley
Were now told how they could dress
The right to walk around unveiled
They'd no longer possess

No more music, no more dancing,
No more shaving of one's beard
The life that once had been in Swat
Had fully disappeared

And for Kainat, just a little girl,
The most affecting rule
Was a ban the Taliban imposed
Forbidding girls from school

From the places where their dreams could grow
And their passions could ignite;
How could adults steal that from them?
It surely was not right

*  *  *

Yet a wrong, once it is spotted,
Doesn't simply go away
Justice must be fought for
Or its opposite can stay

And so Kainat and her schoolmates,
Though of punishment were scared,
Grasped that to defend their rights
Was a duty they all shared:

To stand up to the Taliban
And reject its fearsome creed
But if they'd raise their voices
Would one girl among them lead?

And if one girl's voice was amplified
Who would that one girl be?
Who would become the eyes through which
Their lives the world would see?

"I'll do it," Kainat's schoolmate said
  At her father's slight appeal
"I'll write about the things I see
  The feelings that I feel"

This schoolmate named Malala
  For the BBC would write
In diary-form, she'd tell the world
  About Swat's troubled plight

Of her life as an eleven-year-old
  In the midst of seventh grade,
Of what it meant to live a life
  Unceasingly afraid

"There's fighting," she lamented
"Scary nightmares haunt my sleep
  The news we hear of tragedy
  Too often makes us weep

Yet I still can't help imagining
  That our words can light a spark
And help to bring a future light
  To this tragic, present dark"

*  *  *

At the time that she was writing
  Many schoolhouses were bombed
The Taliban had made it clear
  Their views would not be calmed

As the Pakistani Army
  Waged a battle for control;
In combatting the Taliban
  It was clear they had a role

# KAINAT

The fighting would intensify
As thousands were displaced
Forced to flee all that they knew
In hurried, fearful haste

For no one wants to live in fear
And to feel under attack:
Both Kainat and Malala left
Though in time they both came back

Their school was soon reopened
The violence largely waned
Yet progress could not close its eyes
To a problem that remained

In the background still were people
Who believed that here in Swat
Boys alone should go to school
While girls should not be taught

"I'll stand up to that ignorance,"
Malala firmly said
"That girls deserve the right to school
Is a truth that must be spread"

*   *   *

The Taliban took notice
Of this girl who raised her voice
"We can't let this go on," they said
"It seems we have no choice

But to hush those who defy us
It's a lesson we must teach
Voices mustn't challenge
All the values that we preach

# THE BULLET THAT TURNED TO A SPARK

For a voice raised in defiance
Or a pen that dares oppose
Are the deadly weapons aimed at us
By our unenlightened foes

Since Malala is the loudest
We will silence her the first"
Because of her beliefs, they vowed,
With death she'd now be cursed

*　*　*

That a target was upon her head
Malala did not know
Though cautious, she was unafraid
To school and back she'd go

Till one day, on her bus ride home
Where smiles and jokes were swapped
The mood was quickly broken
When the bus she rode was stopped

"Who's Malala?" yelled a gunman's voice
Then a bullet to her head
In shock, most girls upon the bus
Assumed their friend was dead

They were terror-stricken, horrified
Confused, disturbed, distraught
Before more shots were fired
As two more girls were shot

The first, a girl named Shazia,
Was wounded in the arm;
Her shoulder and her hand
Would suffer devastating harm

# KAINAT

The second, bullet-pierced as well,
From this Taliban attack
Was Kainat, who in seconds
Found her world becoming black

*   *   *

When her eyes would soon reopen
And her vitals would revive
She looked around with horror
Yet with thanks to be alive

Shazia, in greater pain,
In time would be okay
Yet what about Malala?
What harm had come her way?

Doctors, first in Pakistan,
Assessed Malala's fate
A long road to recovery
They all knew would await

For Malala had shown up to them
Extremely close to death
A miracle in many ways
That she arrived with breath

She would need the best in treatment
So they soon sent her away
The rehab she required
Would be found in the UK

*   *   *

Kainat remained in Pakistan
With hopes her friend would heal
Though she too faced new hardships
With which she had to deal

# THE BULLET THAT TURNED TO A SPARK

There were bomb blasts near her family home
Of safety, she felt deprived
Clearly, some were angry
That the three girls had survived

And those angry would get angrier
In the weeks and months ahead
For the girls would not be silenced
But would grow in voice instead

The bullets that had pierced them
With the purpose to suppress
Had instead given new power
All three girls would now possess

But Shazia and Kainat
Still In Swat, felt under threat
For their bravery, though widely praised,
Left their enemies upset

So when a boarding school abroad in Wales
Would offer both a spot
Neither could resist the chance
To get away from Swat

Like Malala, they would leave their homes
And once away they'd find
The power that their lives now had
Which now were intertwined

Malala won the Nobel Prize
Her global reach enlarged
While Kainat and Shazia too
With purpose now felt charged

# KAINAT

They would speak up for the voiceless
And share what they had learned
"Education is a right," they said
"Not something to be earned

Some people will deny that right
Or make it hard to gain
The fight for education
Can at times be full of pain

And for girls across the globe like us
The fight is hardest fought;
Gender inequality
Exists not just in Swat

But if girls around the globe persist
And with each other they unite
Each day, our struggle will progress
Until we win this fight"

\* \* \*

Today they keep on fighting
Still committed and resolved
Kainat knows that in this fight
For years, she'll stay involved

Fuelled by memories of life in Swat
Its beauty and its bliss
Its younger years of hopes and dreams
Before all went amiss

Its terror and its violence
Its years when all seemed dark
The bullet that was meant to dim
That instead became a spark

# THE BULLET THAT TURNED TO A SPARK

Kainat holds these memories tightly
As she's guided by their force
Of ample inspiration
They've become her strongest source

As she works for girls around the world
To secure the rights they're due
For their struggles are her struggles
And their stories are hers too

# *Noa*

Noa has no easy answer to the question of where she grew up. Her parents, both from Canada, were possessed of an untiring wanderlust. As they traveled the world, Noa did too; her passport filled with stamps, her mind with memories.

Sometimes, she says, she reminds herself of some of her earliest travel memories just to be re-immersed in the sense of adventure that came with them: the elusive feeling she described as "seeing the world as so completely new." This poem tells the story of those early journeys, the ones that followed, and all that Noa has gained from them along the way.

# The World's Greatest Treasure

"OPEN your eyes to the world young daughter
Open them wide and you'll see
All the places you one day can travel
All the things that you one day can be

It's a wonderful world that surrounds you
For a girl with a curious mind
So open those eyes our young daughter
And the world's greatest treasures you'll find"

\* \* \*

In a city within South Korea
Where her parents were teaching abroad
Noa opened her eyes filled with wonder
And by all that she saw she was awed

For the world to a newly birthed baby
Is a magical, breathtaking place
Her world felt both safe and protected
For she lived in her parents' embrace

Soon her parents completed their teaching
Their Korean stay drew near its end
That they soon would depart Noa's birthplace
Baby Noa could not comprehend

"It's time to go home," they soon told her
Noa didn't yet know what home meant
So with no fuss and zero objection
From Korea, her family went

\* \* \*

# NOA

"Open your eyes to the world young daughter
Open them wide and you'll see
The Canadian town that we come from
Where a child, from now on you'll be

It's a wonderful world that surrounds you
For a fun-loving child to play
So open those eyes our young daughter
And enjoy, for we're back home to stay"

\*   \*   \*

Home was found in Canadian winters
Snow, in blankets, adorning the ground
Ski hills bustling with tourists and locals
Forests ringing with winter's calm sound

Home was found in Canadian summers
On the beach's nearby sandy shores
Home was found in the school Noa went to
And the aisles of Main Street's quaint stores

Home was everything Noa desired
It was bliss for a girl, eight-years-old
For her hometown, with all of its quaintness
Held the world for a child to behold

But that year Noa's parents decided
That they yearned to go travel once more
"There's too much in this world filled with beauty"
They both said, "for us not explore"

So with Noa, to India's vastness
They departed to go volunteer
First they went for three weeks on a short trip;
Two years later, they went for a year

# THE WORLD'S GREATEST TREASURE

"That our daughter will miss one whole school year
  We're aware but we're not too concerned
  From the world not the class," said her parents
"We believe the best lessons are learned"

\* \* \*

"Open your eyes to the world young daughter
  Open them wide and you'll see
  Little houses that hang on the hillsides
  Next to fields in which locals pick tea

  It's a wonderful world that surrounds you
  For a girl with a generous heart
  So open those eyes our young daughter
  As your newest adventure will start"

\* \* \*

In the Indian town she arrived to
  Noa opened her eyes to the sight
  Of mountains and markets and saris
  Underneath the sun's luminous light

  All around her were dozens of children
  Playing out on the city's worn streets
  They chased cricket balls up and down alleys
  As some snacked on delectable sweets

  And at first, they seemed not at all different
  Than the kids that back home Noa knew
  A child's a child, she reasoned,
  No matter the things they'd been through

  They behaved with a childlike spirit
  There was mischief and fun in their eyes
  They were silly and fun just like she was
  Filled with wit and with youthful surprise

# NOA

But in terms of material wellness
They had much less than Noa possessed
Their houses were smaller, their meals sometimes sparse
In much shabbier clothes they were dressed

And as Noa would shadow her parents
As they helped out within local schools
She saw kids with a hunger for learning
Who were starved of its requisite tools

Sometimes students would learn without textbooks
Sometimes teachers would teach without chalk
Noa witnessed some classes so crowded
It was hard to hear anyone talk

Yet she witnessed much more than just hardship
And the ways different schools were in need
For she witnessed the fire some students possessed
That would drive them to one day succeed

And she witnessed the town's gracious welcome
How they gave to her family a lot
How they opened their homes and their kitchens
And they did it with no second thought

When it, therefore, came time for departure
Noa struggled to say her goodbyes
For where once she had only seen strangers
She saw family in everyone's eyes

"For your love I am grateful," said Noa
"To this new home, I hope to return
From your kindness and from your compassion
There is more that I know I can learn"

# THE WORLD'S GREATEST TREASURE

Then she left with her parents to travel
Their next stop: Tanzania's vast land
Where within its remarkable nature
One adventure loomed – daring and grand

        \*   \*   \*

Open your eyes to the world young daughter
Open them wide and you'll see
From the roof of the world that we stand on
All the birds that with beauty fly free

It's a wonderful world that surrounds you
At the top of this magical peak
So open those eyes our young daughter
And the world's greatest treasures go seek

        \*   \*   \*

From the top of Mount Kilimanjaro
Noa looked at the plains down below
Then she took in the splendor around her
With its sunlight and glaciers and snow

And she stood there replete with exhaustion
As astonishment coursed through her being
And she realized in that special moment
What exactly it was she was seeing

In the beautiful landscape before her
On a peak that now seemed sacred ground
She had heeded the words of her parents
As a wondrous treasure she'd found

Yet, the view was just one single treasure
Of the many she realized she'd gained
The friendships and lessons and beauty
That the world, in its wonder, contained

# NOA

No X marked the spots they were hidden
No treasure chests locked them inside
They were there for the world to discover
For those living with eyes open wide

They were there in the kindness of strangers
In an Indian town far away
They were there in the smiles of school kids
With whom Noa could happily play

They were there in Canadian winters
Even after the trees had gone bare
They were there in her parents' affections
And their constant expressions of care

And these treasures now gather together
Lending beauty to Noa's young mind
She'll keep searching for more her whole lifetime
For more treasures she knows she will find

# *Arlind*

Arlind grew up in Kosovo. When he was only five years old, the Kosovo War broke out: a brutal war fought between the Federal Republic of Yugoslavia and a Kosovo Albanian resistance guerrilla group called the KLA.

On the day that the war finally ended, Arlind vividly remembers hugging one of the Italian soldiers who had helped liberate his city. "Everyone was on the streets laughing, crying, hugging soldiers," he said. Optimism filled the air.

More than fifteen years later, the optimism that accompanied the end of war has morphed for Arlind into a deeper optimism about the potential for interethnic cooperation in his region. "The younger generation is more open-minded and more influenced by ideas of coexistence and cultural understanding," he believes. This poem, however, tells the story of one of Arlind's many experiences during the war, when it was conflict, not coexistence, that reigned.

# The Nights Now Lent to Nightmares

IN a city of open wounds
And closed borders
Burned-out buildings
And long forgotten dreams

In a house not yet abandoned
Where the soundtrack of war plays on repeat
Night after night
A boy hides in the basement
Cloaked in a darkness he hopes makes him invisible

He plays a mortal game of Hide and Seek
His breath held tightly
Trapped in the shrinking space that the world allows him
Hoping it will shrink no further

No one has told him why he must hide
Or who will come and find him
He does not understand the rules of this game
Nor why he has to play
He is only five years old

When he is told, he runs to other basements
Wraps himself in their darknesses
Waits in their windowless eternities
Not knowing for what

Sometimes he sees the adults with him
Folded into themselves
Until they too take little space
Their words say all will be okay
Their faces say the opposite

And in this life on hold
The boy
Though unaware why bedtime now takes place in darkened
  cellars
Why wake-ups often cannot wait until the morning
Why night, which once was host to dreams now lends itself to
  nightmares
Can only wish
To one day be tucked in once more
To blankets
Meant to warm him
Not to hide him

# Arudi

Arudi grew up in Nairobi, Kenya, before moving to New York to spend a year and a half there during high school. "I like to say that America is the place where I discovered race," she says. In Kenya, a country whose population is almost entirely black, there was very little consciousness of racial identity. "Then you move to America and it's sort of like a label is put on you: 'You're black,'" Arudi explains. Suddenly, there were standardized tests commanding her to bubble in her racial identity. There were neighborhoods that seemed to have invisible walls, dividing them on lines of race. And there was also a brewing protest movement, demanding racial justice for African Americans across the country.

This poem tells the story of how Arudi dealt with her newfound racial consciousness, and of how she became involved in the Black Lives Matter movement during her year in New York.

## The Crowd That Spoke For Justice

A maze of people line the street
A traffic jam of souls
A tangle of humanity
With dreams and fears and goals

To each other, they're mere obstacles
Their stories: afterthoughts
To the penthouse-dwelling locals
They are little more than dots

In a human game of pinball
Each one pushed and shoved and knocked;
Seeing everyone but no one too
New Yorkers swiftly walked

\* \* \*

Within these throngs, Arudi walked
Nairobi-born and raised
In a way that only new eyes can
The city, she appraised

Its billboards flashed with glitzy lights
Its buildings bathed in sheen
The city felt as if awake
On mountains of caffeine

As it moved and hummed and bustled
At a nauseously fast pace;
For many on the city's streets
Their walks appeared a race

But the girl walked at a normal speed
As she took the city in
If New York was indeed a race
She was happy not to win

\*   \*   \*

Just months before, she sat at home
When her mother one day said
"It's time for an adventure
To New York I'd like to head"

"It will let you and your sister
See a world you've never seen
Ride its subways, see its landmarks
Taste its myriad cuisines

And the time is now to do this
For with a job there I've been graced
I promise, too, we won't stay long
Just enough to get a taste"

"I'm excited," said Arudi
Nerves eclipsed by mounting glee
The New York, she expected, though
She'd learned of from TV

Where its glamor seemed to trickle down
To all within its midst
The television USA
Appeared by fortune kissed

\*   \*   \*

When she got there, she would quickly learn
That TV spins a tale
Sometimes, in its potency,
On truth it puts a veil

As she slipped into a life
With fewer privileges and perks
Than the ones she'd had in Kenya
With their special Kenyan quirks:

The apartment she now lived in
Felt to her as if compressed
Back home, her family's house was large
And a garden it possessed

There were cars there in the driveway,
In New York, she took the train
From luxuries that once she'd had
She'd now have to abstain

And though others in the city
Suffered more from being poor
Arudi started seeing flaws
Beneath New York's allure

For although within its towers
Were the worlds of the elite
Life was very different
From the viewpoint of the street

\*   \*   \*

Minorities seemed hardest hit
Most likely to be poor
Their lives within the city
Seemed by far the least secure

For the first time in Arudi's life
Her blackness took on weight
She was trapped like all who shared her race
In its disempowered state

# ARUDI

She could see the city's prejudice
And its hidden social code;
An explosive racial dynamite
Could at any time explode

*   *   *

Having seen the seeds of chaos
Arudi could not close her eyes
She now heard the sounds of power
Next to justice-seeking cries

Her heart filled up with empathy
She now pondered what to do
The city had transformed her
As her social conscience grew

Her restless mind grew certain
That the time to act was now:
But to help the city's neediest
She'd first need to learn how

For passion needs direction
Just as action first needs thought
Arudi knew to make a change
She'd first need to be taught

How to organize and advocate
In fighting social ills
No doubt to her, pursuing change
Required special skills

*   *   *

In the city was a summer camp
That claimed to teach those skills
"Our program," its brochure announced
"In young women instills

A keen sense of empowerment
That for leaders is essential
In six short weeks, our girls will learn
The scale of their potential"

"I must attend," Arudi thought
This is surely what I need
"It's here," she said with eagerness
I will gain the skills to lead"

*   *   *

At the camp, she found community
In her mentors and her peers
A shining hope outshone the doubt
That had plagued New York for years

The doubt proclaimed that poverty
Would always live by wealth
The doubt alleged no remedy
To an ailing racial health

The hope proclaimed equality
Would one day live by all
The hope proclaimed that racist walls
If chipped, could one day fall

And Arudi knew instinctively
As she yearned to raise her voice
That hope was all that she possessed
Hope was not a choice

*   *   *

To the city, though, it seemed it was
And it seemed in short supply
As if the city tried its best
Then gave up with a sigh

# ARUDI

Schools for New York's poorest kids
Each year remained abysmal
Graduation rates were weak
Test scores often dismal

And while many labored bravely
In attempts to intervene
The poverty appeared entrenched
The racism routine

Yet, the status quo would tremble
Then a new hope would awaken;
An event on New York's Staten Island
Would leave the city shaken

A black man selling cigarettes
By police was choked to death
"I can't breathe," his final words
Before his final breath

Yet, as his voice extinguished
A thousand others rose
They'd chorus for equality
Injustice they'd oppose

Against poverty and racism
Each voice tinged with indignation
Arudi watched as others learned
The language of frustration

She was fluent in this language
But she spoke it streaked with hope
For anger without vision
Never helps a people cope

# THE CROWD THAT SPOKE FOR JUSTICE

With their sorrows or indignities
With their anguish or their pain
Hope, Arudi reasoned,
Was how anger stayed humane

The anger spoke in protests
That erupted on the streets
Arudi raised awareness
Writing Facebook posts and tweets

To the protests, she would lend her voice
"Black lives matter," her refrain
With courage, she did all she could
For this civil rights campaign

And as elders saw a teenage girl
With such hope in her voice
They couldn't help but realize too
To hope was not a choice

But a duty that they exercised
To fight the nation's wrongs
There was beauty in the voices
Of New York's protesting throngs

\* \* \*

One winter's night, a crowd grew large
Arudi in its midst
She sought to speak for justice
And to passively resist

Against laws she felt were biased
Against charges never pressed
Against sentences that fit no crime
And prejudiced arrests

# ARUDI

As she wandered through the protest
She took all its details in
The sight of all the protesters
Gave goose bumps to her skin

For to the penthouse-dwelling locals
They may still have looked like dots
Yet, their stories, as they told them,
Were no longer afterthoughts

But the basis of their struggles
Of their passion to march on
Of a new age of equality
They hoped to be the dawn

And Arudi looked around and saw
A truth that long she'd known
In a crowd infused by justice
No one person stands alone

# *Killaq*

Killaq grew up in the city of Iqaluit, in northern Canada. She grew up in an indigenous community, a member of the Inuit people, one of Canada's three aboriginal groups. Sometimes, the tension between traditional culture and modernity pulled her in opposite directions. She remembers a moment from her early childhood, sitting with her grandfather, when she gave him a book to read to her. She was shocked when he couldn't read it. The book was in English; her grandfather only reads Inuktitut, the Inuit native language.

Though Killaq speaks some Inuktitut and her grandfather speaks some English, Killaq often thinks about the language barrier between them. "We could never talk in a language we were both comfortable in," she acknowledges with a hint of sadness. Just two generations apart, their worlds are in some ways rapidly diverging.

This poem, imagined in Killaq's voice, tells the story of this intergenerational tension, of the richness of her indigenous identity, and of the ongoing struggle to preserve it in the face of modernity.

# The Answer in the Stars

I wake up at the crack of dawn
The Sun climbs into place
The lights of earth are turned back on
The nighttime leaves no trace

I hear the sound of beating drums
Beneath a stirring song
To spring, the winter now succumbs
We've waited for it long

An igloo's built to mark the day
A dog sled race departs
Artists' crafts are on display
A seal hunt shortly starts

With smiles wide, young children play
About their roots they learn
Our festival is underway
To mark the Sun's return

And as we praise our shining Sun
And all that it brings forth
In ceremony and in fun
We celebrate the North

* * *

The Sun shines down across the land
And lends the earth a glow
Our landscape is both sparse and grand
The "land of ice and snow"

The day is cloaked in mild haze
Then midday's sounds awaken
Upon our land, with love I gaze
Its majesty I take in

# THE ANSWER IN THE STARS

I've skated on our frozen bay
On hidden trails I've walked
I wonder what this land would say
If only nature talked

But though it does not speak in words
I sense its pulsing spirit
In whistling winds and chirping birds
I feel that I can hear it

\*   \*   \*

My forebears heard this land before
They knew the earth as friend
They learned its legends and its lore
To all its needs they'd tend

Upon this earth, they danced and sang
They kayaked on our waters
Their stories, with great passion rang
Out to their sons and daughters

And in their footsteps I now tread
The trail they blazed is mine
The tales they told are far from dead
With wisdom, they still shine

But the tales are now less often told
Losing strength in passing years
We're farther from the world of old
And our trail is stained with tears

For assimilation's forces
In ways subtle and overt
Have, for us, been constant sources
Of a long enduring hurt

# KILLAQ

I see the hurt from where I stand
Today's joy can't conceal it
Its landmarks dot our treasured land
And I can sometimes feel it

I feel it in our elders' pain
Who watch their language languish
I see it in those who complain
Of crippling mental anguish

I hear it in the baby's cries
With not enough to eat
I sense it in the mom who tries
But fails to make ends meet

I smell it in the scent of booze
That's shattered many lives
I hear it in the whispered news
Of husbands beating wives

I sense it in the nurse's yawn
Who's worked too long a shift
I see it in the boy withdrawn
Who school has set adrift

I read it in our textbooks
That speak little of our past
I perceive it in perplexed looks
Over why we've been harassed

And I'm troubled by this gnawing hurt
 I see from where I stand
Its paradox I can't avert
As I look upon our land

# THE ANSWER IN THE STARS

For today's a day of celebration
And so I stand confused;
I see a land of inspiration
But also how it's bruised

And I wonder what my forebears
In their wisdom, would have felt
If they spoke to us, their modern heirs,
What advice would they have dealt?

I wonder but I do not know
What my ancestors would say
What wisdom, nurtured long ago
Would they share with us today?

I think about it all day long
As the afternoon wears on
The celebration ends its song
Its crowds are quickly gone

I watch the sun begin to set
As colors blend and fuse
It's clear that dusk and night have met
In awe-inspiring hues

And as I watch the sun descend
I'm blanketed by dark
The night consumes the daytime's end
And puts out daytime's spark

But a million stars dance in the night
Across our vast, clear sky
And in their sparkling scattered light
Is written a reply

## KILLAQ

To my question of my forebears
Over what advice they'd give:
In a world of joys mixed with despairs
How are we supposed to live?

And the answer I see in the stars
As they glisten and shine bright
Is that even in a world of scars
One can choose to see the light

For although some nights, the stars will hide
In hiding, they're still there
It's light we must take as our guide
For light defeats despair

# *Josef*

Josef grew up in the Czech Republic. He is of Roma ethnicity, a persecuted minority group within the country. Throughout his childhood, he often felt victimized by ethnic discrimination. He still has memories of the day when, while walking home from his soccer practice, a group of older boys in the neighborhood accosted and beat him. The beating left Josef in the hospital for a full week; he insists that he was targeted primarily on the basis of his ethnic identity. When he eventually took his story to the police, the legal system failed to help him. His attackers were never punished. This poem tells the story of how that incident and other encounters with discrimination have shaped Josef's aspirations for the future.

# The Road to Equality

A young man has a dream to be a lawyer
For he has seen the law when misapplied
Distorted from defender to destroyer
Of people's rights and of their ethnic pride

Though some will say the world bends towards justice
Though some will say that truth always prevails
From what he's seen the young man does not trust this
Justice, he believes, unfought for, fails

For justice sometimes looks to him like power
Perverted by the strong to rule the weak
To sit upon their thrones for one more hour
So that their interests stay the ones that speak

And so the young man dreams that when he's older
He'll challenge power's natural drive for more
The weight of change is one he yearns to shoulder
To find the weak a voice with which to roar

He knows it will not be an easy journey
Change tends to travel at a glacial pace
But maybe, when he's one day an attorney
His home's injustice he will help erase

# *Warsan*

Warsan grew up in Somaliland, a self-declared state, viewed internationally as an autonomous region of Somalia. When she was in primary school, she noticed that in many of the local schools, boys outnumbered girls. "It wasn't because teachers wanted more boys," she said; it was because parents cared more about sending their sons to school than sending their daughters. Some days, walking around the city, she noticed government posters aimed at encouraging girls to stay in school and graduate. The posters were an important beginning in the battle for gender equality, she acknowledged, but the preferential treatment of boys in her society is deep-rooted. This poem tells the story of Warsan's birth, and the powerful statement her father made in challenging those entrenched prejudices.

## The Blessing in a Name

A girl is born
And those around her hold their breaths
For she is not a boy

She has two older sisters
Who too failed to come into the world
The way it seemed to want them
And no brothers
Formed to best fit in
To a country shaped for men

Her father is not there to see
His son-to-be
Arrive a daughter

He is abroad
And so the news
That weighs on all who know it
Must be sent to him
Across the globe

The news is written in a letter
Then sealed within an envelope
A dispatch of a disappointed dream
Or so the senders
All believe

But in return
A letter comes
And two short words
Jump out at all who read it

# THE BLESSING IN A NAME

War San
It says
In scrawled Somali script
"Good news" is its translation

The father
In his words
Does not want only
To inform his family of his own contented soul
But to inform his country
That this daughter of Somaliland
Would not be best a son
And so, he asks
To take his blessing
And to gift it to his daughter as her name
A name that knows
A girl born to a world
That does not mold itself to her
Can always mold the world herself
Re-carve its shifting boundaries
And go past its furthest known frontiers
Where she
Like an explorer
Will lay claims
To worlds unknown

# Dahjuanna

Dahjuanna grew up in Flint, Michigan, though she has spent time living in Grand Blanc, a nearby suburb, as well. Drive between the two, she says, and the difference is staggering. "Flint is one of the poorest, most violent cities [in America]," Dahjuanna acknowledges, a claim borne out by United States crime statistics. "And then you have Grand Blanc," she explains, a community that she describes as significantly safer and more affluent than Flint.

Yet, despite the suburban comforts of Grand Blanc, it's in Flint that Dahjuanna finds herself most comfortable. She is not ignorant of Flint's dangers, nor is she naïve about the countless drawbacks of living in a city so deeply affected by poverty. But, in her words, "underneath it all, it's like a big family." This poem tells the story of that "big family": of Dahjuanna's childhood in Flint and the challenges she has faced, but also of the moments of tremendous hope she has experienced in a city in flux.

# The Stage Where Beauty Lives

Auto plants are booming
As a city grows and thrives
Attracting people to it
Who all dream of prosperous lives

Of a house, a car, and savings
Of an income that pays well
Flint appears the place to find it
As far as they can tell

For no worker can imagine
Jobs might one day move away
It seems that all they yearn for
Is here in Flint to stay

But one day, plants begin to close
Conveyor belts shut down
The writing on the wall appears
Of a soon-to-be ghost town

And as jobs are slowly sent abroad
Locals start to get the hint
The glory days they'd lived through
Are about to end in Flint

Some start to leave their homes behind
Their optimism sinks
They give up on their city
And its population shrinks

Its tax base is diminished
Some parks are made to close
If times will ever turn around
Nobody in Flint knows

# DAHJUANNA

But not all locals leave their homes
Since a home is hard to leave
In a brighter, stronger future Flint
Many choose to still believe

*   *   *

Within this city filled with change
A baby's life begins
Dahjuanna comes into the world
The elder of two twins

 Her birth, as does her sister's,
To her parents brings bright light
In a city oft-reminded
Of its crime rate and its blight

But her parents, only teenagers,
Who seemed a perfect fit
As time goes by grow distant
And then, one day, they split

In the aftermath, her father leaves
For a military stint;
Dahjuanna and her twin are left
With just their mom in Flint

*   *   *

Her mother does the best she can
To keep her household stable
But even with her loving heart
She often is not able

For it's hard to clothe and care and feed
And do it on one's own
Poverty is hard to fight
And hardest-fought alone

# THE STAGE WHERE BEAUTY LIVES

Some days hard feels impossible
And in moments of such weight
When Dahjuanna sees her mom engulfed
By a foggy, darkened state

She prepares herself to leave her home
Together with her twin
To their grandma's nearby house they both
Like times before move in

When her dad moves back years later
She too sometimes lives with him
Her life's lived in transitions
In a city sometimes grim

No one school in which she's rooted
No one address, no one bed
No one home in which to store her life
But changing ones instead

And it isn't just her home in flux
But the people that pass through
The faces seen upon Flint's streets
Are often changing too

Some fall victim to these lethal streets
To its gangs and drugs and crime
Some are locked up inside prisons
Trapped in worlds of stolen time

And in weeping homes on weeping streets
Sit devastated mothers
Fathers cry out for their sons
While sisters cry for brothers

# DAHJUANNA

Dahjuanna cries among them
She can feel these families' fears
For her uncle, just sixteen years old,
Is locked up for ten years

All these tears course through the city
Like a stream of what's been lost
That flows as long as violence does
And gathers up its cost

*   *   *

Yet within this stream of sorrow
Dahjuanna finds a place
To seek refuge from the currents
In a less tempestuous space

Safe from all the city's dangers
From its violence and its rage
Is a world of possibility
Upon a theater's stage

On this stage, Dahjuanna starts to act
Breathing life into her roles
The theater is a therapy
For her city's weary souls

For the stage is where these weary souls
See worlds unlike their own
In different plays in different ways
New dreams are being shown

But they also see their world onstage
For their neighbors are the cast
On stage it seems their pain dissolves
It's hope, not hurt, that's vast

## THE STAGE WHERE BEAUTY LIVES

In this hope is a reminder
To Dahjuanna and the crowd
Of the talent in their city
Of a reason to be proud

Of the music next to gunshots
Of the joy beside despair
Of the people in a changing world
That for their city care

Of the beauty and the love that lives
Beneath their city's rage
Of the dreams that can be chased and reached
Beyond the theater's stage

# Sofiya

Sofiya grew up in a small town called Zalishchyky in the Ukraine. Not too far away is the city of Lviv, the largest in Western Ukraine. In the summer of 2014, Sofiya had the chance to visit Lviv. She was instantly enamored by it. More than anything else, she loved the narrow lively streets lined with little shops in the center of the city. "You can see street musicians playing, you can see local art and architecture, you can see local artists selling pictures they painted," she enthused. The streets overflowed with life.

Fast-forward one year and the streets of Ukraine had a very different energy to them. A revolution, sparked in February 2014, led to the ouster of the Ukrainian president. In response, Russia deployed troops to the eastern part of Ukraine, igniting what became known as the Crimean Crisis, a battle for territorial control of a region called Crimea, previously recognized as part of the Ukraine. Tension pervaded the whole country, and the life that once abounded on Ukraine's streets was now sometimes overshadowed by the death that the conflict was creating. This poem speaks to that shadow of death by telling the story of Sofiya's experiences watching a funeral procession in her hometown.

## The Sidewalk Stained with Tears

HUNDREDS stand
Upon a tear-stained sidewalk

As a funeral procession passes by
As young and old alike both cry
As silences resound with "why?"

For in the coffin lies a boy
Just twenty-three years old

The mourners say the boy was brave –
To fear, he would not be a slave
For freedom's call his life he gave

But death cares not
Whether this boy was bold

&ast; &ast; &ast;

A teenage girl stands in the crowd
Tears in her eyes, head gravely bowed
Of country both repulsed and proud

This is the first time
She has lived with war

Her father is a region priest
He'll bless the boy by war deceased
And mourn the fighting in the East

The girl has seen her father
Grieve before

&ast; &ast; &ast;

# SOFIYA

She knows this death won't be the last
The drums of war have not yet passed
Its hurt and loss grows deep and vast

More boys costumed as men
Will come back dead

The leaders will debate and stall
In safety, far from battle's call
In offices, as young boys fall

Claimed not as loss
But sacrifice instead

\*   \*   \*

These deaths the girl cannot ignore
She sees the coffin built of war
That holds a boy she'll see no more

She weeps to see a too-young life
Passed on

For this boy to her has a name
Her town's the town from which he came
His death feels more than warfare's game

He is her classmate's brother
Ever gone

\*   \*   \*

The girl's tears turn to silent pain
Yet, somehow, sparks of hope remain
That in her homeland of Ukraine

The peace she used to know
Will soon return

That one day on this grieving street
The gathered crowd will once more meet
In joy at violence's defeat

And celebrate the home
For which they yearn

# Elias

Elias was born in a Tanzanian refugee camp called Mishamo. In 1993, his family repatriated to their homeland of Burundi, but only a month after arriving, civil war broke out. By 1996, Elias left Burundi and moved to a refugee camp in Tanzania; by then he had already lost his parents, elder brothers, and a sister.

In 2004, he left Tanzania and moved back to Burundi, but would only stay there briefly. The UN camp he was staying at in Burundi was attacked, and so he fled to a new refugee camp in Malawi. At the camp in Malawi, food was rationed on a monthly basis. The rations were far from abundant. Nevertheless, when some of the locals in Malawi from outside of the camp, who had even less food than the camp residents, came to the camp desperately asking for help, Elias was quick to share his rations. "I would give what I had, regardless of thinking that I'm not going to make it these thirty days," Elias explained. "As I grew as an orphan, I grew up with the mentality of mutualism," he said, defining mutualism as the idea of helping and caring for one another.

In the refugee camp, Elias's ultimate dream was to one day leave to get an education abroad. This poem captures a moment in his life in the camp, imagining this dream.

## The World Beyond the Fences

A young man
The age of an old boy
Sits in a refugee camp
In a world between two worlds
A rest stop for the weary
As he climbs
From the depths of his memories
To the heights of his dreams
That float just beyond his reach

In this holding pen of possibility
The young man watches
As ghosts of their former selves walk by
Doctors and storekeepers
Teachers and taxi-drivers
Mothers and daughters
Of disparate worlds
And of the same
All brought together
By misfortune's inclusivity

In their faces
The young man sees all that has been lost
In hollowed eyes
Aching to be filled with the sights of serenity
In anxious ears
Too used to the sounds of danger
In empty mouths
Hungering for the warmth of a home-cooked meal

# ELIAS

And in these faces etched with loss
In wrinkles not of age but of experience
The young man sees a pain he knows
For he's endured the losses of a lifetime
Of his parents
And his homeland
And the little hope
That still believed that life was fair

But yet
For all that he has seen the world behind him
He cannot tear his eyes away
From the future's blinding brightness
From a world that has no fences
From horizons that do not fill up
With the faces of yesterday's pain

He dreams of these horizons
Of the places he will one day go
And in these dreams he travels
Not the travels of a refugee
Not the searching steps
That tread for solid ground on which to stand
But the travels of a voyager
The knowing steps
That leave their mark
And do not quickly fade

# Lobsang

Lobsang grew up in a small village in Tibet. "The lifestyle was really simple," she recalled, reminiscing about the summer flowers, mountain air, and countless farms that dotted the landscape. When she was only eight years old, Lobsang's parents decided to send her away from Tibet to Dharamsala, the home of the Tibetan government-in-exile located in India, where they believed better opportunities awaited her. This poem captures the story of her journey.

# The Long Walk Through the Night

A girl says goodbye to her mom and her dad
Not knowing when they'll reunite
She's too young to feel anything other than sad
As she's pushed from her life to take flight

Her parents respond, both with somber goodbyes,
Yet it's they who have told her to go
Her journey, they grasp, is a grave enterprise
But necessity sometimes risks woe

"Go forward," they say to their daughter, just eight,
"When you're older, you will understand
 Why we send you today to a far-away fate
 But ourselves cannot come hold your hand"

"Go forward," they say, "to a world where you'll grow"
 She is far too young not to adhere
"Go forward," they say, "to a world that we know
 Holds more for you than you'll find here

\* \* \*

Her father's goodbye for one month stretches out
For he takes her and finds her a guide
In the city of Lhasa, where trust wrestles doubt,
His intentions, in secret, must hide

Till the day that he leaves with a kiss and a smile
 Though with fear he by now has been struck
"Sometimes," he imparts, "home is found in exile"
"I love you my daughter – good luck"

\* \* \*

94

# THE LONG WALK THROUGH THE NIGHT

The girl sees him go, yet he stays in her mind
He will live there, though miles away
The girl then prepares for the dangers she'll find
As she goes with her guide on their way

There are borders that bisect the journey that waits
She must travel through forests and peaks
To Nepal and then onward through India's gates
To the exiled home that she seeks

She is given new clothes to put on as disguise
Travel's safer in Nepalese dress
With no visa, she yearns to steer clear of all eyes
That could cause to her journey distress

"We must walk in the dark," she is told by her guide
"We'll be helped by the cover of night
For the guards that look for us with eyes open wide
After nightfall are robbed of their sight"

"Even though you are scared," her guide tells her with care
"You're the bravest girl I've ever met —
Hold on to your courage — I know that it's there
On this journey away from Tibet"

*   *   *

The girl does her best to be brave and be strong
But some nights, she can't hold back her tears
The walking is tiring and painful and long
And what passes in days feels like years

Some nights, while she walks, she is pounded by rain
As she treks through a forest of mud
She is bitten by insects again and again
That latch on to her skin and suck blood

She is haunted by grief over all that she's left
She is fearful of what lies ahead
Of her friends and her family she wanders bereft
Into nights that are heavy with dread

And she wishes her parents were there by her side
It's their love that she craves above all
Yet as she laments, she is told by her guide:
"We have made it across to Nepal"

*   *   *

Upon reaching Nepal, by her aunt she's received
She is welcomed with warmth and with cheer
"Dear girl," she is told, "you must feel quite relieved
To have made it in safety to here"

"Here's a warm meal to eat, here are new clothes to wear"
Says her aunt, "Take a moment to rest"
"Then once you awaken, I'll help you prepare
For the very last step of your quest"

That step takes the girl to a refugee center
Where she gathers the papers she needs
To India, she can now legally enter
To her exiled home, she proceeds

*   *   *

She finally reaches her journey's conclusion
Where a new journey's waiting to start
She rests for a moment, consumed by confusion,
Emotions run wild in her heart

# THE LONG WALK THROUGH THE NIGHT

It's too soon to make sense of the path she's traversed
Only time will give questions replies
In worlds of uncertainty she's been immersed
And she's lived them through eight-year-old eyes

She is miles away from her parents' warm hugs
Their goodbyes are still etched in her brain
Next to frightening nights filled with bloodsucking bugs
And an eight-year-old refugee's pain

But for all that she's burdened by memory's weight
She looks to the future that comes
For all that she pities her exiled state
The future, with hopefulness, hums

# *Uddhav*

Uddhav grew up in Kathmandu, Nepal. Towards the end of high school, he moved to Hong Kong to complete his education at the United World College located there. In his first year in Hong Kong, on April 25, 2015, an enormous earthquake struck Nepal. In the hours and days that followed, Uddhav watched helplessly from afar, as media reports documented the death and devastation in his beloved home country. Alongside those reports, though, were also stories of hope: of neighbors doing all that they could to help each other through an incredibly trying time, embodying the sense of solidarity that Uddhav long had felt in his country.

This poem tells Uddhav's story of growing up in Kathmandu, and tells the story of the 2015 earthquake and the fear and hope that has followed.

## The Palace Built From Heartbreak

LEGEND says a snake-filled lake
Once covered Kathmandu
A holy man arrived one day
And saw the water's blue

He drew his sword and cut a gorge
The waters quickly drained
The snakes were ridded of their home
That long had been maintained

And so the snakes grew angry
Their King rose up incensed
"For the home that we have lost," he said
"We must be recompensed"

In little time, the day arrived
When a new lake was created
For the snakes and for their Serpent King
A new home now awaited

And the humans who together dwelled
On the new lake's outer shore
Built the King an underwater palace
Of jewels and rich décor

To the locals, the King promised
Generations of protection
In return they would not touch his lake
In its blissful, calm perfection

From a moment in which all was lost
The serpents' fate had turned
From tragedy can come rebirth
The Serpent Kingdom learned

*   *   *

# UDDHAV

Around two thousand years ago
Where the drained lake once had been
Legend says a city rose
And people flooded in

Homes were built and temples founded
Cultures formed, though some would fade,
Leaders rose and leaders fell
And, yet, the city's spirit stayed

Its history unfolded
Like an ever-growing book
Full of wisdom and of insight
To which its residents could look

And as years went by the city
Watched its old mix with its new;
The past and present blended
Into modern Kathmandu

*   *   *

In this city lived a young boy
And the boy's name was Uddhav
There was much about his hometown
That the boy grew up to love

He loved standing on his rooftop
Where he could see his city sprawl
He adored the smells and tastes of home
The steaming rice with dal

He loved looking at the mountains
That surrounded Kathmandu
How the sun would duck behind them
And each morning rise anew

# THE PALACE BUILT FROM HEARTBREAK

He excited over holidays
In their myriad delights
He looked forward to Diwali
Hindus' festival of lights

And above all else, he loved the care
That people showed each other
Even strangers in his country
In Nepali, he'd call brother

\* \* \*

Yet, for all he loved his country
When a special chance appeared
To complete his high school years abroad
In a high school much revered

He decided he would take it
For most chances don't come twice;
To Uddhav, this school appeared to be
A students' paradise

And he figured in his time away
Not much would change at all
In his much beloved Kathmandu
And all throughout Nepal

\* \* \*

No forewarning could have readied him
For how wrong he soon would be
When the future took a shocking turn
From hope to tragedy

In a moment of great magnitude
A major earthquake struck;
It was only the beginning
Of Kathmandu's tragic luck

# UDDHAV

From abroad, Uddhav observed the news
In a helpless state of shock
A hopeless wish arose in him
To turn back nature's clock

For the present that the news revealed
Was filled with fear and dread
His country's heart stood broken
As it gathered up its dead

Many landmarks of his childhood
Were now reduced to rubble
It pained him to see photos
Of his countrymen in trouble

But within these haunting photographs
Unfiltered of their grief
Uddhav could see a people
Who would fight to find relief

In their eyes, he could see heroism
Shining through their tears
He could see in them a courage
That would overcome their fears

He could hear it in his parents' voices
When he reached them on the phone
Saying, "We are here, we are in pain
But we are not alone"

Though we know there will be aftershocks
On land and in our hearts
It is now we will begin to heal
It is now rebuilding starts"

\* \* \*

# THE PALACE BUILT FROM HEARTBREAK

The rebuilding's only just begun
It declares no certain end
Uddhav, like others, is aware
For years it will extend

Like the serpents in their darkest hour
Uprooted from their lake
There are many still without a home
In the earthquake's tragic wake

With no underwater palace yet
Of jewels and rich décor
To return them to the lives they lived
In the Earthquake's Great Before

But a message from the serpents' tale
May help them as they cope
From tragedy can come rebirth
In darkness, there's still hope

# Conclusion

THE final school that I visited as part of my project was UWC Waterford Kamhlaba in Swaziland, a small landlocked country bordered by South Africa and Mozambique. The school was opened in 1963 as a multi-racial school: a bold statement of opposition to South Africa's apartheid policies. As South Africa was building walls between people, Waterford decided it would build bridges.

I found it appropriate to end my project travels at Waterford: a school that to this day stands as a symbol of hope's enormous power. When others were seeing the world as it was, Waterford's founder chose instead to see the world as it could ideally be. That quality – of seeing the world in its promise not only in its problems – is the quality I've endeavored to share through this collection. The students at Waterford embodied this quality, and so too did the hundreds of other students I met throughout my journey.

In 1990, Nelson Mandela, recently released from prison, first visited Waterford. If anyone was able to see the world as it could be, not just as it was, it was Mandela, and so it was fitting for him to visit a school whose mission so deeply aligned with his own. He knew the school from before – two of his daughters had attended while he was in prison on Robben Island – and he would get to know the school better in the years to come – many of his grandchildren would attend, and he himself, in 1995, would become the UWC movement's co-president.

I imagine what that visit must have been like – that first encounter between a man so committed to the ideals of peace and racial justice and a school living out those very ideals. It must have been a celebration of hope – Mandela gifting the campus with his extraordinary vision, as the students gifted him their youthful optimism in return. It must have been a celebration of courage – of Mandela's unwavering belief in a better tomorrow. But it also must have been a celebration of stories: of Mandela's story, of Waterford's story, but also of the remarkable personal stories each and every student carried with them.

# CONCLUSION

For me, this entire journey has been a celebration of stories. From my early visit to Wales where I met Mira in the beautiful castle by the sea, to my final project visit to Swaziland, every step of my journey was inspired by the stories that surrounded me. This collection bears witness to those stories that I was privileged to gather, and to one insight I was reminded of again and again throughout my travels; even a small story can hold within it vast amounts of hope.

## The Hope That Lights the Future

HOPE is the future in color
When others see just black and white
Hope is the sun rising warmly
At the end of a cold winter's night

Hope is the voice that says maybe
When the whole world appears to say no
Hope is the laugh of a baby
Who still sees the world in its glow

Hope is the day after heartbreak
When a nation makes no room for fear
Hope is the end of the tunnel
Unseen, but eternally near,

Hope is the prayer of the yearning
That seeks, in its plea, to be heard
Hope is despair overturning
As a dream is no longer deferred

Hope is the restless desire
For tomorrow to outshine today
Hope is the spark of a fire
That lights for all dreamers the way

And it lives in the soul, not in hiding,
But in waiting to one day be found;
Search within, and when you surely find it
Let its light and its spirit abound

# *Acknowledgments*

To the uwc principals, administrators, and faculty members who welcomed me into their communities and offered me assistance, I am eternally grateful. Special thank yous to Libby Mason, Heather Gross, David Hawley, Benoît Charlebois, Kim Mulder, Deanna Cuthbert, Danielle Pope, Hayley Goldberg, Arnett Edwards, Christian Bock, Laurence Nodder, Helen White, Julia Angsterberger, Peter Howe, Tian Bersey, John Walmsley, Julie Harris, Nick Lush, Tom Oden, Naomi Swinton, Jennifer Rowland, Stephen Lowry, and Helene Caillet, for all of their help, big and small.

To Shelby Davis and Phil Geier, thank you for believing in this project and for all of your support in enabling it to become a reality.

To the wonderful, warm, and friendly students, who shared their stories with me, without you this book would not be possible; your kindness and relentless optimism has taught me so much.

To all those who helped in the editing process, thank you for your insights and your time.

To my incredible book designer, Ben Denzer, thank you for your hard work and your tremendous creative vision.

And, most of all, to my amazing family and friends, thank you for your constant encouragement and support along this journey.

Made in the USA
Columbia, SC
26 May 2018